EAVAN BOLAND

THE JOURNEY
and other poems

CARCANET

ARLEN
HOUSE
The Women's Press

First published in 1987 by
Carcanet Press Limited
208-212 Corn Exchange Buildings
Manchester M4 3BQ
and 198 Sixth Avenue
New York, NY 10013
and in 1986 by Arlen House
Kinnear Court
16/20 Cumberland Street South
Dublin 2
Republic of Ireland

British Library Cataloguing in Publication Data
Boland, Eavan
 The journey and other poems.
 I. Title
 821'.914   PR6052.03/

 ISBN 0-85635-683-2
 ISBN 85132 005 9 p/b
 ISBN 85732 004 0 cloth

The Publisher acknowledges financial assistance
from the Arts Council of Great Britain

Typeset in 10pt Palatino by Bryan Williamson, Manchester
Printed in England by SRP Ltd., Exeter

The Journey
and Other Poems

For my Mother

Acknowledgements

Acknowledgements are made to the editors of the following publications in which some of these poems appeared:

The Irish Times; the Irish Press; An Gael; The Salmon; Poetry Ireland; RTE Radio I; RTE Television; BBC Radio 3; The Poetry Review; PN Review; Rubicon; Verse; The Midland Review; Northwest Review; Chicago Review; Ontario Review; The American Poetry Review; Seneca Review.

The poem *The Journey* appeared in limited edition, published by Deerfield/Gallery.

I wish to thank the Irish-American Cultural Foundation for their award in 1983 and the Irish Arts Council for their bursary in 1985.

CONTENTS

I

II

III

I

I Remember

I remember the way the big windows washed
out the room and the winter darks tinted
it and how, in the brute quiet and aftermath,
an eyebrow waited helplessly to be composed

from the palette with its scarabs of oil
colours gleaming through a dusk leaking from
the iron railings and the ruined evenings of
bombed-out, post-war London; how the easel was

mulberry wood and, porcupining in a jar,
the spines of my mother's portrait brushes
spiked from the dirty turpentine and the face
on the canvas was the scattered fractions

of the face which had come up the stairs
that morning and had taken up position in
the big drawing-room and had been still
and was now gone; and I remember, I remember

I was the interloper who knows both love and fear,
who comes near and draws back, who feels nothing
beyond the need to touch, to handle, to dismantle it,
the mystery; and how in the morning when I came down –

a nine-year-old in high, fawn socks –
the room had been shocked into a glacier
of cotton sheets thrown over the almond
and vanilla silk of the French Empire chairs.

Mise Eire

I won't go back to it –

my nation displaced
into old dactyls,
oaths made
by the animal tallows
of the candle –

land of the Gulf Stream,
the small farm,
the scalded memory,
the songs
that bandage up the history,
the words
that make a rhythm of the crime

where time is time past.
A palsy of regrets.
No. I won't go back.
My roots are brutal:

I am the woman –
a sloven's mix
of silk at the wrists,
a sort of dove-strut
in the precincts of the garrison –

who practises
the quick frictions,
the rictus of delight
and gets cambric for it,
rice-coloured silks.

I am the woman
in the gansy-coat
on board the "Mary Belle",
in the huddling cold,

holding her half-dead baby to her
as the wind shifts East
and North over the dirty
water of the wharf

mingling the immigrant
guttural with the vowels
of homesickness who neither
knows nor cares that

a new language
is a kind of scar
and heals after a while
into a passable imitation
of what went before.

Self-Portrait on a Summer Evening

Jean-Baptiste Chardìn
is painting a woman
in the last summer light.

All summer long
he has been slighting her
in botched blues, tints,
half-tones, rinsed neutrals.

What you are watching
is light unlearning itself,
an infinite unfrocking of the prism.

Before your eyes
the ordinary life
is being glazed over:
pigments of the bibelot,
the cabochon, the water-opal
pearl to the intimate
simple colours of
her ankle-length summer skirt.

Truth makes shift:
The triptych shrinks
to the cabinet picture.

Can't you feel it?
Aren't you chilled by it?
The way the late afternoon
is reduced to detail –

the sky that odd shape of apron –

opaque, scumbled –
the lazulis of the horizon becoming

optical greys
before your eyes
before your eyes
in my ankle-length
summer skirt

crossing between
the garden and the house,
under the whitebeam trees,
keeping an eye on
the length of the grass,
the height of the hedge,
the distance of the children

I am Chardin's woman

edged in reflected light,
hardened by
the need to be ordinary.

The Oral Tradition

I was standing there
at the end of a reading
or a workshop or whatever,
watching people heading
out into the weather,

only half-wondering
what becomes of words,
the brisk herbs of language,
the fragrances we think we sing,
if anything.

We were left behind
in a firelit room
in which the colour scheme
crouched well down –
golds, a sort of dun

a distressed ochre –
and the sole richness was
in the suggestion of a texture
like the low flax gleam
that comes off polished leather.

Two women
were standing in shadow,
one with her back turned.
Their talk was a gesture,
an outstretched hand.

They talked to each other
and words like "summer"
"birth" "great-grandmother"
kept pleading with me,
urging me to follow.

"She could feel it coming" –
one of them was saying –
"all the way there,
across the fields at evening
and no one there, God help her

"and she had on a skirt
of cross-woven linen
and the little one
kept pulling at it.
It was nearly night . . ."

(Wood hissed and split
in the open grate,
broke apart in sparks,
a windfall of light
in the room's darkness)

". . . when she lay down
and gave birth to him
in an open meadow.
What a child that was
to be born without a blemish!"

It had started raining,
the windows dripping, misted.
One moment I was standing
not seeing out,
only half-listening

staring at the night; the next
without warning
I was caught by it:
the bruised summer light,
the musical sub-text

of mauve eaves on lilac
and the laburnum past
and shadow where the lime
tree dropped its bracts
in frills of contrast

where she lay down
in vetch and linen
and lifted up her son
to the archive
they would shelter in:

the oral song
avid as superstition,
layered like an amber in
the wreck of language
and the remnants of a nation.

I was getting out
my coat, buttoning it,
shrugging up the collar.
It was bitter outside,
a real winter's night

and I had distances
ahead of me: iron miles
in trains, iron rails
repeating instances
and reasons; the wheels

singing innuendoes, hints,
outlines underneath
the surface, a sense
suddenly of truth,
its resonance.

Fever

is what remained or what they thought
remained after the ague and the sweats
were over and the shock of wild flowers
at the bedside had been taken away;

is what they tried to shake out of
the crush and dimple of cotton,
the shy dust of a bridal skirt;
is what they beat, lashed, hurt like

flesh as if it were a lack of virtue
in a young girl sobbing her heart out
in a small town for having been seen
kissing by the river; is what they burned

alive in their own back gardens
as if it were a witch and not the full-
length winter gaberdine and breathed again
when the fires went out in charred dew.

My grandmother died in a fever ward,
younger than I am and far from
the sweet chills of a Louth spring –
its sprigged light and its wild flowers –

with five orphan daughters to her name.
Names, shadows, visitations, hints
and a half-sense of half-lives remain.
And nothing else, nothing more unless

I re-construct the soaked-through midnights;
vigils; the histories I never learned
to predict the lyric of; and re-construct
risk; as if silence could become rage,

as if what we lost is a contagion
that breaks out in what cannot be
shaken out from words or beaten out
from meaning and survives to weaken

what is given, what is certain
and burns away everything but this
exact moment of delirium when
someone cries out someone's name.

The Unlived Life

"Listen to me" I said to my neighbour,
"how do you make a hexagon-shape template?"

So we talked about end papers,
cropped circles, block piece-work
while the children shouted and
the texture of synthetics as compared
with the touch of strong cloth
and how they both washed.

"You start out with jest so much caliker" –
Eliza Calvert Hall of Kentucky said –
"that's the predestination
but when it comes to cuttin' out
the quilt, why, you're free to choose".

Suddenly I could see us
calicoed, overawed, dressed in cotton
at the railroad crossing, watching
the flange-wheeled, steam-driven, iron omen
of another life passing, passing
wondering for a moment what it was
we were missing as we turned for home

to choose
in the shiver of silk and dimity
the unlived life, its symmetry
explored on a hoop with a crewel needle
under the silence of the oil light;

to formalize the terrors of routine
in the algebras of a marriage quilt
on alternate mornings when you knew
that all you owned was what you shared.

It was bed-time for the big children
and long past it for the little ones
as we turned to go
and the height of the season went by us;

tendrils, leaps, gnarls of blossom,
asteroids and day-stars of our small world,
the sweet-pea ascending the trellis
the clematis descended
while day backed into night
and separate darks blended the shadows,
singling a star out of thin air

as we went in.

Lace

Bent over
the open notebook –

light fades out
making the trees stand out
and my room
at the back
of the house, dark.

In the dusk
I am still
looking for it –
the language that is

lace:

a baroque obligation
at the wrist
of a prince
in a petty court.
Look, just look
at the way he shakes out

the thriftless phrases,
the crystal rhetoric
of bobbined knots
and bosses:
a vagrant drift
of emphasis
to wave away an argument
or frame the hand
he kisses;
which, for all that, is still

what someone
in the corner
of a room,
in the dusk,
bent over
as the light was fading

lost their sight for.

The Bottle Garden

I decanted them – feather mosses, fan-shaped plants,
asymmetric greys in the begonia –
into this globe which shows up how the fern shares
the invertebrate lace of the sea-horse.

The sun is in the bottle garden,
submarine, out of its element
when I come down on a spring morning;
my sweet, greenish, inland underwater.

And in my late thirties, past the middle way,
I can say how did I get here?
I hardly know the way back, still less forward.
Still, if you look for them, there are signs:

Earth stars, rock spleenwort, creeping fig
and English ivy all furled and herded
into the green and cellar wet
of the bottle; well, here they are

here I am a gangling schoolgirl
in the convent library, the April evening outside,
reading the *Aeneid* as the room darkens
to the underworld of the Sixth book –

the Styx, the damned, the pity and
the improvised poetic of imprisoned meanings;
only half aware of the open weave of harbour lights
and my school blouse riding up at the sleeves.

Suburban Woman: a Detail

I

The chimneys have been swept.
The gardens have their winter cut.
The shrubs are prinked, the hedges gelded.

The last dark shows up the headlights
of the cars coming down the Dublin mountains.

Our children used to think they were stars.

II

This is not the season
when the goddess rose
out of seed, out of wheat,
out of thawed water
and went, distracted and astray,
to find her daughter.

Winter will be soon:
Dun pools of rain;
ruddy, addled distances;
winter pinks, tinges and
a first-thing smell of turf
when I take the milk in.

III

Setting out for a neighbour's house
in a denim skirt,

a blouse blended in
by the last light,

I am definite
to start with
but the light is lessening,
the hedge losing its detail,
the path its edge.

Look at me, says the tree.
I was a woman once like you,
full-skirted, human.

Suddenly I am not certain
of the way I came
or the way I will return,
only that something
which may be nothing
more than darkness has begun
softening the definitions
of my body, leaving

the fears and all the terrors
of the flesh shifting the airs
and forms of the autumn quiet

crying "remember us".

The Briar Rose

Intimate as underthings
beside the matronly damasks –

the last thing
to go out at night
is the lantern-like, white insistence
of these small flowers;

their camisole glow.

Standing here on the front step
watching wildness break out again

it could be
the unlighted stairway,
I could be
the child I was, opening

a bedroom door
on Irish whiskey, lipstick,
an empty glass,
oyster crepe-de-Chine

and closing it without knowing why.

The Women

This is the hour I love: the in-between,
neither here-nor-there hour of evening.
The air is tea-coloured in the garden.
The briar rose is spilled crepe-de-Chine.

This is the time I do my work best,
going up the stairs in two minds,
in two worlds, carrying cloth or glass,
leaving something behind, bringing
something with me I should have left behind.

The hour of change, of metamorphosis,
of shape-shifting instabilities.
My time of sixth sense and second sight
when in the words I choose, the lines I write,
they rise like visions and appear to me:

women of work, of leisure, of the night,
in stove-coloured silks, in lace, in nothing,
with crewel needles, with books, with wide open legs

who fled the hot breath of the god pursuing,
who ran from the split hoof and the thick lips
and fell and grieved and healed into myth,

into me in the evening at my desk
testing the water with a sweet quartet,
the physical force of a dissonance –

the fission of music into syllabic heat –
and getting sick of it and standing up
and going downstairs in the last brightness

into a landscape without emphasis,
light, linear, precisely planned,
a hemisphere of tiered, aired cotton,

a hot terrain of linen from the iron,
folded in and over, stacked high,
neatened flat, stoving heat and white.

Nocturne

After a friend has gone I like the feel of it:
The house at night. Everyone asleep.
The way it draws in like atmosphere or evening.

One-o-clock. A floral teapot and a raisin scone.
A tray waits to be taken down.
The landing light is off. The clock strikes. The cat

comes into his own, mysterious on the stairs,
a black ambivalence around the legs of button-back
chairs, an insinuation to be set beside

the red spoon and the salt-glazed cup,
the saucer with the thick spill of tea
which scalds off easily under the tap. Time

is a tick, a purr, a drop. The spider
on the dining room window has fallen asleep
among complexities as I will once

the doors are bolted and the keys tested
and the switch turned up of the kitchen light
which made outside in the back garden

an electric room – a domestication
of closed daisies, an architecture
instant and improbable.

The Fire in Our Neighbourhood

The sign factory went on fire last night.
Maybe "factory" is too strong a word.
They painted window-signs there when times
were good, wooden battens, glass, plaster-board.

The paint cans went off like rifle fire.
By the time we heard sirens we were standing
at the windows watching ordinary things –
garden walls, pools of rain – reflecting

violent ornamentation,
our world grown elaborate as if
down-to-earth cloth and wood became
gimp and tatting, guipure and japanning.

Familiar figures became curious shadows.
Everyday men and women were the restless
enigmatic shapes behind glass.
Then the sirens stopped; the end began.

It didn't take long. The fire brigade
turned their hoses on the sawmills where
the rock band practises on Saturdays
with the loud out-of-tune bass guitar.

And the flames went out. The night
belonged to the dark again, to the scent
of rain in the air, to its print on the pavement
and the neighbours who slept through the excitement.

On Holiday

Ballyvaughan.
Peat and salt.
How the wind bawls
across the mountains,
scalds the orchids
of the Burren.

They used to leave milk
out once on these windowsills
to ward away
the child-stealing spirits.

The sheets are damp.
We sleep between the blankets.
The light cotton of the curtains
lets the light in.

You wake first thing
and in your five-year-size
striped nightie you are
everywhere trying everything:
the springs on the bed,
the hinges on the window.

You know your a's and b's
but there's a limit now
to what you'll believe.

When dark comes I leave
a superstitious feast
of wheat biscuits, apples,
orange juice out for you
and wake to find it eaten.

Growing Up
from Renoir's drawing: "Girlhood"

Their two heads, hatted, bowed, mooning
above their waist-high tides of hair
pair hopes.
           This is the haul and full
of fantasy:
           full-skirted girls,
a canvas blued and empty with the view
of unschemed space and the anaemic
quick of the pencil picking out
dreams blooding them with womanhood.

They face the future. If they only knew!

There in the distance, bonnetted,
round as the hairline of a child –
indefinite and infinite with hope –
is the horizon, is the past and all
they look forward to is memory.

There and Back

Years ago I left the guest-house
in the first September light
with no sense
I would remember this:

starting up the engine
by the river, picking up
speed on the road
signposted Dublin,

measuring Kilkenny, Carlow, Naas
as distances not places,
yearning for my own
version of the world

every small town was
taking down
its shutters to
and I was still miles from;

until I shut the car door sharp
at eight years ago and you were
with the children,
with their bottles,

at your heels, the little radiances
of their faces turned up,
heliotropic,
to our kiss.

The Wild Spray

It came to me one afternoon in summer –
a gift of long-stemmed flowers in a wet
contemporary sheath of newspapers
which pieced off easily at the sink.

I put them in an ironstone jug
near the window; now years later
I know the names for the flowers
they were but not the shape they made:

The true rose beside the mountain rose,
the muslin finery of asparagus fern,
rosemary, forsythia; something about it was
confined and free in the days that followed

which were the brute, final days of summer –
a consistency of milk about the heat haze,
midges freighting the clear space between
the privet and the hedge, the nights chilling

quickly into stars, the morning breaking late
and on the low table the wild spray
lasted for days, a sweet persuasion,
a random guess becoming a definition.

I have remembered it in a certain way –
displaced yellows and the fluencies
of colours in a jug making a statement of
the unfurnished grace of white surfaces

the way I remember us when we first came here
and had no curtains; the lights on the mountain
that winter were sharp, distant promises
like crocuses through the snowfall of darkness.

We stood together at an upstairs window
enchanted by the patterns in the haphazard,
watching the streetlamp making rain into
a planet of tears near the whitebeam trees.

II

The Journey

for Elizabeth Ryle

Immediately cries were heard. These were the loud wailing of infant souls
weeping at the very entrance-way; never had they had their share of life's
sweetness for the dark day had stolen them from their mothers' breasts
and plunged them to a death before their time.
– Virgil, The Aeneid, Book VI

And then the dark fell and "there has never"
I said "been a poem to an antibiotic:
never a word to compare with the odes on
the flower of the raw sloe for fever

"or the devious Africa-seeking tern
or the protein treasures of the sea-bed.
Depend on it, somewhere a poet is wasting
his sweet uncluttered metres on the obvious

"emblem instead of the real thing.
Instead of sulpha we shall have hyssop dipped
in the wild blood of the unblemished lamb,
so every day the language gets less

"for the task and we are less with the language."
I finished speaking and the anger faded
and dark fell and the book beside me
lay open at the page Aphrodite

comforts Sappho in her love's duress.
The poplars shifted their music in the garden,
a child startled in a dream,
my room was a mess –

the usual hardcovers, half-finished cups,
clothes piled up on an old chair –
and I was listening out but in my head was
a loosening and sweetening heaviness,

not sleep, but nearly sleep, not dreaming really
but as ready to believe and still
unfevered, calm and unsurprised
when she came and stood beside me

and I would have known her anywhere
and I would have gone with her anywhere
and she came wordlessly
and without a word I went with her

down down down without so much as
ever touching down but always, always
with a sense of mulch beneath us,
the way of stairs winding down to a river

and as we went on the light went on
failing and I looked sideways to be certain
it was she, misshapen, musical –
Sappho – the scholiast's nightingale

and down we went, again down
until we came to a sudden rest
beside a river in what seemed to be
an oppressive suburb of the dawn.

My eyes got slowly used to the bad light.
At first I saw shadows, only shadows.
Then I could make out women and children
and, in the way they were, the grace of love.

"Cholera, typhus, croup, diptheria"
she said, "in those days they racketed
in every backstreet and alley of old Europe.
Behold the children of the plague".

Then to my horror I could see to each
nipple some had clipped a limpet shape –
suckling darknesses – while others had their arms
weighed down, making terrible pietàs.

40

She took my sleeve and said to me, "be careful.
Do not define these women by their work:
not as washerwomen trussed in dust and sweating,
muscling water into linen by the river's edge

"nor as court ladies brailled in silk
on wool and woven with an ivory unicorn
and hung, nor as laundresses tossing cotton,
brisking daylight with lavender and gossip.

"But these are women who went out like you
when dusk became a dark sweet with leaves,
recovering the day, stooping, picking up
teddy bears and rag dolls and tricycles and buckets –

"love's archaeology – and they too like you
stood boot deep in flowers once in summer
or saw winter come in with a single magpie
in a caul of haws, a solo harlequin".

I stood fixed. I could not reach or speak to them.
Between us was the melancholy river,
the dream water, the narcotic crossing
and they had passed over it, its cold persuasions.

I whispered, "let me be
let me at least be their witness," but she said
"what you have seen is beyond speech,
beyond song, only not beyond love;

"remember it, you will remember it"
and I heard her say but she was fading fast
as we emerged under the stars of heaven,
"there are not many of us; you are dear

"and stand beside me as my own daughter.
I have brought you here so you will know forever
the silences in which are our beginnings,
in which we have an origin like water,"

and the wind shifted and the window clasp
opened, banged and I woke up to find
the poetry books stacked higgledy piggledy,
my skirt spread out where I had laid it –

nothing was changed; nothing was more clear
but it was wet and the year was late.
The rain was grief in arrears; my children
slept the last dark out safely and I wept.

Envoi

It is Easter in the suburb. Clematis
shrubs the eaves and trellises with pastel.
The evenings lengthen and before the rain
the Dublin mountains become visible.

My muse must be better than those of men
who made theirs in the image of their myth.
The work is half-finished and I have nothing
but the crudest measures to complete it with.

Under the street-lamps the dustbins brighten.
The winter flowering jasmine casts a shadow
outside my window in my neighbour's garden.
These are the things that my muse must know.

She must come to me. Let her come
to be among the donnée, the given.
I need her to remain with me until
the day is over and the song is proven.

Surely she comes, surely she comes to me –
no lizard skin, no paps, no podded womb
about her but a brightening and
the consequences of an April tomb.

What I have done I have done alone.
What I have seen is unverified.
I have the truth and I need the faith.
It is time I put my hand in her side.

If she will not bless the ordinary,
if she will not sanctify the common,
then here I am and here I stay and then am I
the most miserable of women.

III

Listen. This is the Noise of Myth

This is the story of a man and woman
under a willow and beside a weir
near a river in a wooded clearing.
They are fugitives. Intimates of myth.

Fictions of my purpose. I suppose
I shouldn't say that yet or at least
before I break their hearts or save their lives
I ought to tell their story and I will.

When they went first it was winter; cold,
cold through the Midlands and as far West
as they could go. They knew they had to go –
through Meath, Westmeath, Longford,

their lives unravelling like the hours of light –
and then there were lambs under the snow
and it was January, aconite and jasmine
and the hazel yellowing and puce berries on the ivy.

They could not eat where they had cooked,
nor sleep where they had eaten
nor at dawn rest where they had slept.
They shunned the densities

of trees with one trunk and of caves
with one dark and the dangerous embrace
of islands with a single landing place.
And all the time it was cold, cold:

the fields still gardened by their ice,
the trees stitched with snow overnight,
the ditches full; frost toughening lichen,
darning lace into rock crevices.

And then the woods flooded and buds
blunted from the chestnut and the foxglove
put its big leaves out and chaffinches
chinked and flirted in the branches of the ash.

And here we are where we started from –
under a willow and beside a weir
near a river in a wooded clearing.
The woman and the man have come to rest.

Look how light is coming through the ash.
The weir sluices kingfisher blues.
The woman and the willow tree lean forward, forward.
Something is near; something is about to happen;

something more than Spring
and less than history. Will we see
hungers eased after months of hiding?
Is there a touch of heat in that light?

If they stay here soon it will be summer; things
returning, sunlight fingering minnowy deeps,
seedy greens, reeds, electing lights
and edges from the river. Consider

legend, self-deception, sin, the sum
of human purpose and its end; remember
how our poetry depends on distance,
aspect: gravity will bend starlight.

Forgive me if I set the truth to rights.
Bear with me if I put an end to this:
She never turned to him; she never leaned
under the sallow-willow over to him.

They never made love; not there; not here;
not anywhere; there was no winter journey;
no aconite, no birdsong and no jasmine,
no woodland and no river and no weir.

Listen. This is the noise of myth. It makes
the same sound as shadow. Can you hear it?
Daylight greys in the preceptories.
Her head begins to shine

pivoting the planets of a harsh nativity.
They were never mine. This is mine.
This sequence of evicted possibilities.
Displaced facts. Tricks of light. Reflections.

Invention. Legend. Myth. What you will.
The shifts and fluencies are infinite.
The moving parts are marvellous. Consider
how the bereavements of the definite

are easily lifted from our heroine.
She may or she may not. She was or wasn't
by the water at his side as dark
waited above the Western countryside.

O consolations of the craft.
How we put
the old poultices on the old sores,
the same mirrors to the old magic. Look.

The scene returns. The willow sees itself
drowning in the weir and the woman
gives the kiss of myth her human heat.
Reflections. Reflections. He becomes her lover.

The old romances make no bones about it.
The long and short of it. The end and the beginning.
The glories and the ornaments are muted.
And when the story ends the song is over.

An Irish Childhood in England: 1951

The bickering of vowels on the buses,
the clicking thumbs and the big hips of
the navy-skirted ticket collectors with
their crooked seams brought it home to me:
Exile. Ration-book pudding.
Bowls of dripping and the fixed smile
of the school pianist playing "Iolanthe",
"Land of Hope and Glory" and "John Peel".

I didn't know what to hold, to keep.
At night, filled with some malaise
of love for what I'd never known I had,
I fell asleep and let the moment pass.
The passing moment has become a night
of clipped shadows, freshly painted houses,
the garden eddying in dark and heat,
my children half-awake, half-asleep.

Airless, humid dark. Leaf-noise.
The stirrings of a garden before rain.
A hint of storm behind the risen moon.
We are what we have chosen. Did I choose to? –
in a strange city, in another country,
on nights in a North-facing bedroom,
waiting for the sleep that never did
restore me as I'd hoped to what I'd lost –

let the world I knew become the space
between the words that I had by heart
and all the other speech that always was
becoming the language of the country that
I came to in nineteen-fifty-one:
barely-gelled, a freckled six-year-old,
overdressed and sick on the plane
when all of England to an Irish child

was nothing more than what you'd lost and how:
was the teacher in the London convent who
when I produced "I amn't" in the classroom
turned and said – "you're not in Ireland now".

Fond Memory

It was a school where all the children wore darned worsted;
where they cried – or almost all – when the Reverend Mother
announced at lunch-time that the King had died

peacefully in his sleep. I dressed in wool as well,
ate rationed food, played English games and learned
how wise the Magna Carta was, how hard the Hanoverians

had tried, the measure and complexity of verse,
the hum and score of the whole orchestra.
At three-o-clock I caught two buses home

where sometimes in the late afternoon
at a piano pushed into a corner of the playroom
my father would sit down and play the slow

lilts of Tom Moore while I stood there trying
not to weep at the cigarette smoke stinging up
from between his fingers and – as much as I could think –

I thought this is my country, was, will be again,
this upward-straining song made to be
our safe inventory of pain. And I was wrong.

Canaletto in the National Gallery of Ireland

Something beating in
making pain and attention –
a heat still
livid on the skin
is the might-have-been:

the nation, the city
which fell
for want of
the elevation in
this view of the Piazza,

its everyday light
making it everyone's
remembered city:
airs and shadows,
cambered distances.

I remember
a city like this –
the static coral
of reflected brick
in its river.

I envy these
pin-pointed citizens
their solid ease,
their lack of any need
to come and see

the beloved republic
raised
and saved
and scalded into
something measurable.

The Emigrant Irish

Like oil lamps we put them out the back,

of our houses, of our minds. We had lights
better than, newer than and then

a time came, this time and now
we need them. Their dread, makeshift example.

They would have thrived on our necessities.
What they survived we could not even live.
By their lights now it is time to
imagine how they stood there, what they stood with,
that their possessions may become our power.

Cardboard. Iron. Their hardships parcelled in them.
Patience. Fortitude. Long-suffering
in the bruise-coloured dusk of the New World.

And all the old songs. And nothing to lose.

Tirade for the Lyric Muse

You're propped and swabbed and bedded.
I could weep.
There's a stench of snipped flesh
and tubed blood.
I've come to see if beauty is skin deep.

Mongrel features.
Tainted lint and cotton.
Sutures from the lip to ear to brow.
They've patched your wrinkles
and replaced your youth.
It may be beauty
but it isn't truth.

You are the victim of a perfect crime.
You have no sense of time.
You never had.
You never dreamed he could be so cruel.
Which is why you lie back
shocked in cambric,
slacked in bandages
and blubbing gruel.
My white python writhing your renewal!

I loved you once.
It seemed so right, so neat.
The moon, the month, the flower, the kiss –
there wasn't anything that wouldn't fit.
The ends were easy
and the means were short
when you and I were lyric and elect.
Shall I tell you what we overlooked?

You in this bed.
You with your snout,
your seams, your stitches
and your sutured youth.

You,
you with your smocked mouth
are what your songs left out.

We still have time.
Look in the glass.
Time is the flaw.
Truth is the crystal.

We have been sisters
in the crime.
Let us be sisters
in the physic:

Listen.
Bend your darned head.
Turn your good ear.
Share my music.

The Woman takes her Revenge on the Moon

Claret. Plum. Cinnabar.
The damask of the peach.
The flame and sweet
carmine of late berries.
The orchard colours of the morning –

I am learning them.
I streak ochres on my cheeks.
This is my make-up box.
This is how I own
the tone secrets of the dawn.

It takes skill
to make my skin
a facsimile
of absolute light,
of scarlet turning into carmine.

Once I start
I lose all sense
of time, of space,
of clarity, of will.
I mix to kill.

Orange madder.
The magenta tint.
I am perfecting it.
It must be excellent
or she won't fall for it.

I fresh the pearly wet
across my face.
I rouge the flesh.
I spread and flush the red.
The trap is set.

I walk out
in the evening air.
Early, early
in the clear evening.
I raise my head like a snare.

There it is.
I can feel it –
the pleasure of it! –
the dun slither,
the hysteric of her white

expression, its surprise
as she drowns,
as she douses
in my face,
in my sunrise.

The Glass King

Isabella of Bavaria married Charles VI of France in 1385. In later years his
madness took the form of believing he was made from glass.

When he is ready he is raised and carried
among his vaporish plants; the palms and ferns flex;
they almost bend; you'd almost think they were going to kiss him;
and so they might; but she will not, his wife,

no she can't kiss the lips in case he splinters
into a million Bourbons, mad pieces.
What can she do with him – her daft prince?
His nightmares are the Regency of France.

Yes, she's been through it all, his Bavaroise,
blub-hipped and docile, urgent to be needed –
from churching to milk fever, from tongue-tied princess
to the queen of a mulish king – and now this.

They were each other's fantasy in youth.
No splintering at all about that mouth
when they were flesh and muscle, woman and man,
fire and kindling. See that silk divan?

Enough said. Now the times themselves
are his asylum: these are the Middle Ages, sweet
and savage era of the saving grace; indulgences
are two a penny; under the stonesmith's hand

stone turns into lace. I need his hand now.
Outside my window October soaks the stone;
you can hear it; you'd almost think
the brick was drinking it; the rowan drips

and history waits. Let it wait. I want
no elsewheres: the clover-smelling, stove-warm
air of Autumn catches cold; the year turns;
the leaves fall; the poem hesitates:

If we could see ourselves, not as we do –
in mirrors, self-deceptions, self-regardings –
but as we ought to be and as we have been:
poets, lute-stringers, makyres and abettors

of our necessary art, soothsayers of the ailment
and disease of our times, sweet singers,
truth tellers, intercessors for self-knowledge –
what would we think of these fin-de-siècle

half-hearted penitents we have become
at the sick-bed of the century: hand-wringing
elegists with an ill-concealed greed
for the inheritance?
                              My prince, demented

in a crystal past, a lost France, I elect you emblem
and ancestor of our lyric: it fits you like a glove –
doesn't it? – the part; untouchable, outlandish,
esoteric, inarticulate and out of reach

of human love: studied every day by your wife,
an ordinary honest woman out of place
in all this, wanting nothing more than the man
she married, all her sorrows in her stolid face.